The Essential Guide to Mental Health: How Counseling and Psychiatry Can Change Lives

By: Aaron Esfahani, MSN, APRN, BSBA

Dedication

To God, the ultimate source of strength, wisdom, and grace—thank You for guiding my path and blessing me with purpose.

To my beautiful, loving wife, Erin, whose unwavering support and partnership have enriched every step of this journey. And to my incredible children, Alex and Aleah, you are my joy and inspiration, a daily reminder of life's blessings.

To my mother, whose steadfast encouragement and sacrifices have been a foundation in my life—thank you for always believing in me.

And to my entire family, whose love and support have shaped who I am today. This book is for all of you.

Table of Contents

Introduction

- Why Mental Health Matters for Everyone
- A Look at Stigma and Societal Views
- What to Expect from This Book

Chapter 1: Mental Health Across the Lifespan

- Early Life and Adolescence
- Mental Health in Adulthood and Transition Phases
- Aging and Mental Health Needs in Later Years

Chapter 2: Understanding Counseling – More Than Just Talking

- The Purpose and Process of Counseling
- Types of Counseling Approaches
- Benefits of Counseling Beyond Crisis Management

Chapter 3: Psychiatry as a Tool for Healing

- What is Psychiatry?
- Key Roles of Psychiatry in Mental Health Care
- Types of Psychiatric Medications and Their Uses

Chapter 4: Lifestyle Factors and Holistic Approaches to Mental Health

- Introduction to Lifestyle and Mental Health
- Nutrition and Mental Health
- Physical Activity and Its Impact on Mental Health

Chapter 5: Building Strong Support Systems: The Role of Relationships in Mental Health

- Understanding the Types of Supportive Relationships
- The Benefits of Strong Support Systems
- How to Build and Strengthen Support Systems

Chapter 6: Therapeutic Interventions and Their Transformative Power

- The Foundation of Psychotherapy: Understanding the Basics
- Cognitive Behavioral Therapy (CBT): Changing Thoughts and Behaviors
- Dialectical Behavior Therapy (DBT): Balancing Acceptance and Change

Chapter 7: The Role of Medication in Mental Health Treatment

- The Purpose and Scope of Psychiatric Medication
- Types of Psychiatric Medications and Their Functions
- Considerations When Starting Medication

Appendix

- Mental Health Resources and Hotlines
- Further Reading and Educational Resources
- Self-Assessment Tools for Personal Growth

Introduction

In my career as an advanced practice nurse and mental health advocate, I've had the privilege of leading one of the most successful mental health practices in Georgia. This work has been both profoundly challenging and deeply rewarding, as I've dedicated myself to helping others reach their highest potential. As a man of faith, a devoted husband, a father, and a person with a genuine love for others, I've come to see mental health not as an isolated issue but as an essential part of human dignity and well-being.

I believe that all people deserve a chance to function at their best, to overcome the pain and challenges that can weigh heavily on their lives. But over the years, I have also witnessed the immense suffering that can undermine a person's mental health. I've seen children scarred by neglect, adolescents grappling with the lasting effects of abuse, and adults burdened by trauma that sometimes goes back decades. The mental health conditions that arise from physical and sexual abuse, and from abandonment and neglect, are not just diagnoses in a textbook; they are the heartbreaking realities that so many people live with each day.

In this work, I am called by God to help others, driven by a deep-seated belief in the power of compassion and understanding. My faith has guided me to advocate for those who feel unseen, unheard, or misunderstood. As a Christian, I feel a responsibility to extend love and healing wherever I can and to encourage others to seek the help they need to find peace and restoration. Mental health is not simply a matter of addressing symptoms; it is about helping people reclaim their lives and realize the fullness of who they are meant to be.

Writing this book has become an extension of that calling. In *The Essential Guide to Mental Health: How Counseling and Psychiatry Can Change Lives*, my goal is to shed light on the importance of mental health treatment, to break down the barriers of stigma and misconception, and to encourage those who are struggling to seek support. This book is not just for those who are suffering; it is for their families, friends, and communities as well, to equip them with understanding and the tools to help others navigate the journey to wellness.

Mental health is something that affects every person across every stage of life. From children who need stability and care as they grow, to teenagers who are trying to find their way, to adults who shoulder immense responsibilities, and to seniors who face unique challenges in their later years—each phase of life brings its own mental health needs. This book will explore the role that mental health plays in shaping us, often in ways we are not even fully aware of, and it will outline the path to better understanding and supporting mental wellness through counseling, psychiatry, and self-care practices.

I'll begin by discussing the different ways mental health challenges manifest throughout the stages of life, offering a lens through which to understand these experiences as part of a larger journey. From there, I'll dive into what counseling really is—beyond the stigma, beyond the stereotypes—and how it can empower people to heal, grow, and thrive. In subsequent chapters, we will explore the role of psychiatry, a vital medical tool that too often faces misunderstanding, and how it can be combined with counseling for a more holistic approach to care.

In addition to understanding these forms of treatment, knowing when to seek help is one of the most critical parts of the mental health journey. Too often, people wait until a crisis has taken hold before reaching out, so I'll offer practical advice on recognizing the signs that professional support is needed. I'll also explore the impacts of mental health within relationships, at work, and in moments of crisis, where we are reminded that we are never truly alone in our experiences.

At the heart of it all, I hope to offer hope and encouragement. Mental health care is not just about addressing problems; it is about finding resilience, rediscovering joy, and embracing the fullness of life. As I share the knowledge I've gained from my years in practice, my hope is that this book becomes a trusted companion for those seeking support or for those who want to support others in their journey to mental health. Each of us has a role to play, and together, we can work toward a world where mental health is valued, nurtured, and truly understood.

May this book inspire you, whether you're here seeking healing for yourself or wanting to help others find their way. And may you know that the journey to mental wellness is not one you have to walk alone.

Chapter 1: Mental Health Across the Lifespan

Introduction to Mental Health and Development

Mental health isn't static; it shifts and changes along with our circumstances, relationships, and the roles we assume in life. By examining mental health across the lifespan, we can better understand how each stage brings its own challenges and opportunities. Whether we are children learning to navigate the world, teenagers searching for identity, adults balancing responsibilities, or older adults facing transitions, mental health remains a fundamental part of our well-being.

In this chapter, we'll explore these stages, addressing the unique pressures and needs of each and highlighting how early experiences can shape our mental health for years to come. Through this journey, we aim to lay the groundwork for a better understanding of the broad, lifelong impact of mental health.

Mental Health in Early Childhood (Ages 0-10)

In early childhood, the foundations for mental health are laid. During this time, children are shaped by the nurturing they receive from caregivers, their relationships with family, and the environment in which they grow up. Secure attachment and a stable, loving environment can promote healthy development, while neglect or trauma can leave lasting scars.

Key Factors in Early Childhood Mental Health:

- **Attachment and Bonding:** Children need close, responsive caregivers to feel secure and safe. This attachment becomes the foundation for future relationships.

- **Early Trauma and Its Effects:** For some children, early trauma—such as neglect, abuse, or the loss of a parent—can lead to developmental delays, behavioral issues, or attachment disorders. These experiences often manifest as difficulties in trust, emotional regulation, or self-esteem.

- **Building Resilience Through Play and Learning:** Play is a powerful way for young children to explore emotions, build confidence, and develop problem-solving skills. Encouraging imaginative play and social interaction helps children build the resilience they'll need throughout life.

Warning Signs in Childhood: While every child is different, persistent aggression, extreme withdrawal, or a reluctance to interact with others could be early signs of mental health challenges that need attention.

Mental Health in Adolescence (Ages 10-20)

Adolescence is a time of tremendous change. As teenagers seek independence and develop their own identities, they are also navigating emotional highs and lows, social pressures, and significant life transitions. For many, mental health challenges may emerge or intensify during these years.

Key Factors in Adolescent Mental Health:

- **Identity and Self-Esteem:** Adolescents are highly focused on establishing a sense of identity and belonging. Low self-esteem or feeling out of place can exacerbate mental health struggles, especially if teens are bullied or excluded.

- **Influence of Peers and Social Media:** Peer relationships play a critical role in adolescent mental health, but social media has amplified this dynamic. Cyberbullying, unrealistic portrayals of life, and constant comparison can all have negative effects.

- **Common Adolescent Mental Health Issues:** Depression, anxiety, and eating disorders often first appear during adolescence. Risk-taking behaviors, self-harm, and suicidal ideation are also concerns that may arise as teens try to cope with intense emotions or challenging circumstances.

Warning Signs in Adolescence: Symptoms like withdrawing from family and friends, significant changes in behavior, or academic decline can indicate underlying issues. Early intervention, counseling, and strong support systems are essential.

Mental Health in Adulthood (Ages 20-60)

Adulthood is marked by increasing responsibilities, from careers to relationships to family. Many adults experience heightened stress from balancing these demands, and without adequate support, mental health can suffer.

Key Factors in Adult Mental Health:

- **Work-Life Balance and Burnout:** Many adults struggle to find a healthy balance between work, family, and personal time. Chronic stress can lead to burnout, affecting both physical and mental health.

- **Relationships and Family Dynamics:** Marriage, parenthood, and family relationships bring joy but can also create stress. Divorce, loss, and the responsibilities of caregiving can strain mental health and increase the risk of depression or anxiety.

- **Financial and Social Pressures:** Financial concerns and the pressure to "have it all" can fuel anxiety and depression. Adults are also prone to comparison, sometimes feeling that they're falling short in their careers or personal lives.

Common Mental Health Conditions in Adulthood: Depression and anxiety are the most common mental health conditions in this stage, but many adults also struggle with PTSD from earlier traumas. Additionally, issues like addiction, anger, and chronic stress often require professional support.

Warning Signs in Adulthood: When adults begin to feel chronically overwhelmed, irritable, or disconnected from loved ones, it can be a signal to seek help. Recognizing these signs early can make a significant difference.

Mental Health in Later Life (Ages 60 and Above)

In later life, mental health takes on a new dimension as people encounter unique changes and challenges, such as retirement, loss of loved ones, and physical aging. Despite stereotypes, mental health remains just as important in these years as at any other time of life.

Key Factors in Mental Health for Older Adults:

- **Loss, Grief, and Isolation:** Older adults often experience the loss of friends, partners, and family members. Loneliness and isolation are common and can contribute to depression and anxiety.

- **Cognitive Health and Dementia:** Cognitive decline can impact mental health and quality of life. Memory loss, confusion, and other symptoms of dementia can also create emotional distress for both the individual and their loved ones.

- **Maintaining a Sense of Purpose:** For many, retirement and aging can create a sense of purposelessness. Finding ways to remain engaged, whether through volunteering, hobbies, or social activities, can be protective for mental health.

Common Mental Health Issues in Later Life:

Depression and anxiety remain prevalent, though they often go unaddressed in older adults. Dementia, Alzheimer's, and the associated mental and emotional challenges are also key issues that require support.

Warning Signs in Later Life: Withdrawal, lack of interest in previously enjoyed activities, and changes in sleep or appetite are potential indicators that support may be needed. Early intervention can help older adults navigate these changes more comfortably and with dignity.

Conclusion: A Lifelong Approach to Mental Health

Each stage of life presents new mental health challenges and opportunities. By understanding mental health across the lifespan, we can better equip ourselves to support our loved ones and our communities in maintaining wellness at every age. The importance of mental health cannot be overstated—our minds and hearts need nurturing and care throughout our entire lives.

In this book, we'll continue exploring how counseling, psychiatry, and a strong support system can guide us through the inevitable highs and lows. As we delve into the role of mental health care, I hope you'll find encouragement and inspiration to seek wellness not just in times of struggle, but as an ongoing, lifelong journey.

Chapter 2: Understanding Counseling – More Than Just Talking

Introduction to Counseling

When most people think of counseling, they envision someone lying on a couch, sharing their troubles with a silent therapist. But the reality is that counseling is much more dynamic and impactful. It's a guided journey to self-discovery, healing, and personal growth, tailored to meet each individual's unique needs. Counseling is not just about venting frustrations; it's about finding constructive ways to cope with life's challenges, gaining insights into oneself, and ultimately reaching a place of resilience and well-being.

This chapter will explore the true purpose of counseling, introduce some of its most effective approaches, and underscore how counseling can offer life-changing benefits far beyond crisis management.

The Purpose and Process of Counseling

1. Counseling as a Safe Space for Self-Exploration

Counseling provides a confidential, non-judgmental environment where individuals can explore their thoughts, feelings, and behaviors. This safe space encourages honesty, vulnerability, and introspection—elements essential for real change. Here, people can speak openly about challenges, traumas, fears, and hopes without fear of rejection or misunderstanding.

2. Goal-Oriented Nature of Counseling

Counseling is often misunderstood as endless talking with no clear end in sight. In reality, effective counseling is structured around specific goals tailored to each person's needs. Counselors work collaboratively with clients to identify these goals, which might include:

- Improving communication skills

- Managing anxiety or depression

- Healing from past trauma

- Enhancing self-esteem

- Developing healthier relationships

3. The Stages of Counseling: An Overview

Most counseling follows a process that can be broken down into stages:

- **Building Rapport and Trust:** In the initial sessions, the counselor and client work to establish a trusting relationship. Trust is essential, as it allows clients to feel comfortable enough to delve into sensitive issues.

- **Assessment and Goal Setting:** The counselor helps the client articulate their issues and identify specific goals. This stage often involves questionnaires or discussions to get a clearer picture of the client's life.

- **Intervention and Growth:** The bulk of counseling work occurs here, where clients work toward their goals using specific techniques and strategies. This stage can be challenging, as clients confront difficult emotions or memories, but it's also where transformative growth happens.

- **Consolidation and Termination:** Once goals are achieved, the counseling relationship winds down.

The counselor helps the client recognize and consolidate their progress, equipping them with tools to maintain well-being independently.

Types of Counseling Approaches

There is no one-size-fits-all in counseling; different approaches work for different individuals and issues. Here are some of the most common, each with a unique focus and set of techniques:

1. Cognitive Behavioral Therapy (CBT)

CBT is one of the most widely used forms of counseling. It operates on the principle that our thoughts, feelings, and behaviors are interconnected and that by changing our thoughts, we can influence our emotions and actions. In CBT:

- **Core Beliefs and Automatic Thoughts** are examined, helping clients identify and challenge negative patterns.

- **Behavioral Techniques** are used to help clients gradually face and overcome fears.

- **Real-World Application** is emphasized; clients practice new ways of thinking and behaving outside of sessions.

CBT is particularly effective for managing conditions like anxiety, depression, phobias, and PTSD. It empowers clients with tools they can use long after counseling ends.

2. Psychodynamic Therapy

Rooted in Freudian theory, psychodynamic therapy focuses on uncovering unconscious motivations and unresolved conflicts, often stemming from childhood. By exploring these deeply rooted issues, clients gain insight into current behaviors and emotions. In psychodynamic therapy:

- Clients often explore **repressed emotions** and experiences from their past.

- **Free association** is encouraged, allowing thoughts to flow without censorship.

- **Transference**—the projection of feelings onto the therapist—is examined to gain insights into the client's relationships.

This approach is well-suited for those who want to explore their inner world in-depth and understand how past experiences shape current issues.

3. Person-Centered (Rogerian) Therapy

Person-centered therapy, developed by Carl Rogers, is based on the belief that individuals have the capacity for self-healing and personal growth. In this approach, the counselor provides empathy, acceptance, and unconditional positive regard, creating an environment where clients can feel safe to explore their thoughts and feelings. Key elements include:

- **Empathetic Listening:** The counselor listens deeply and reflects the client's thoughts, helping them feel understood and validated.

- **Self-Acceptance:** Clients are encouraged to accept themselves without judgment, laying the groundwork for change.

- **Client Empowerment:** The therapist's non-directive approach helps clients become more self-reliant and confident in their decision-making.

This approach is often used in counseling people dealing with self-esteem issues, relationship difficulties, or emotional challenges.

4. Solution-Focused Brief Therapy (SFBT)

SFBT is a short-term approach that focuses on finding solutions rather than delving into problems. It's ideal for clients seeking immediate, tangible improvements in their lives. Techniques include:

- **Goal Setting:** Clients are encouraged to define clear, achievable goals from the outset.

- **Miracle Questions:** Clients imagine how life would be different if a particular problem was solved.

- **Strength Identification:** Clients are encouraged to recognize their own strengths and successes as tools for future challenges.

SFBT is particularly helpful for clients who are action-oriented and want to see quick results, often in situations involving stress, family issues, or career challenges.

Benefits of Counseling Beyond Crisis Management

Counseling is not only for moments of crisis. Engaging in counseling can lead to personal growth, improved relationships, and greater emotional resilience. Here are some long-term benefits of counseling:

1. Enhanced Self-Awareness

Through counseling, clients gain a deeper understanding of themselves, their motivations, and their reactions to various situations. This self-awareness allows for better decision-making and the ability to break unhealthy patterns.

2. Improved Coping Skills

Life will always have its ups and downs, but counseling equips individuals with coping skills to manage stress, anxiety, and challenges more effectively. These skills can include mindfulness practices, relaxation techniques, and cognitive restructuring.

3. Strengthened Relationships

Counseling can help clients build better communication skills, develop empathy, and set healthy boundaries. Whether it's with family, friends, or colleagues, these improved relational skills can lead to more satisfying and supportive relationships.

4. Building Emotional Resilience

Resilience isn't just about bouncing back from adversity; it's about growing through it. Counseling can help individuals develop resilience by teaching them to embrace change, face fears, and approach challenges with a positive mindset.

Common Misconceptions about Counseling

Despite its benefits, counseling is often misunderstood or stigmatized. Here are some myths and the realities behind them:

1. "Counseling is only for people with serious mental health issues."

- Reality: Counseling is for anyone seeking growth, clarity, or support. Many people in counseling are simply looking to navigate life's challenges in a healthier way.

2. "Counseling is just talking, and it can't really change anything."

- Reality: Counseling is a structured, evidence-based process with proven techniques for helping individuals achieve real change.

3. "Counseling is a sign of weakness."

- Reality: Seeking counseling is a courageous act of self-care. It takes strength to confront difficult issues and work towards self-improvement.

Conclusion: Counseling as a Journey of Transformation

Counseling is more than just talking; it's a journey of personal transformation that helps individuals gain insight, resilience, and hope. By understanding the goals, processes, and various approaches to counseling, we can appreciate its profound impact on mental health and overall well-being. Counseling offers people a way to navigate life's challenges, address deep-seated issues, and ultimately reach their highest potential.

In the chapters ahead, we'll explore how psychiatry and other mental health interventions complement counseling, offering additional tools to support healing. By combining these resources, individuals can experience a more holistic path to mental health and well-being.

Chapter 3: Psychiatry as a Tool for Healing

Introduction to Psychiatry and Mental Health

Psychiatry is a branch of medicine focused on diagnosing, treating, and preventing mental health conditions. While counseling provides emotional support, practical tools, and therapeutic interventions, psychiatry adds a medical dimension to mental health care. This chapter delves into the role of psychiatry, explaining its purpose, key approaches, and how it works alongside counseling to provide comprehensive mental health care.

Psychiatry can often be misunderstood or stigmatized, with myths and fears surrounding medication and psychiatric diagnoses. This chapter aims to clarify what psychiatry truly is, break down common misconceptions, and reveal how psychiatry and counseling together can create powerful, life-changing outcomes for individuals.

What is Psychiatry?

1. Psychiatry as a Medical Discipline

Unlike counseling, which focuses on behavioral and emotional support, psychiatry is a medical field that requires formal training in medicine. Psychiatrists are medical doctors who specialize in mental health. They undergo rigorous medical schooling and residency training that allows them to understand the complex relationship between the mind and body, as well as how various factors—genetics, neurochemistry, environment— contribute to mental health conditions.

2. Understanding the Biopsychosocial Model

Psychiatry often uses the **biopsychosocial model** to understand mental health, viewing it as an interplay of biological, psychological, and social factors:

- **Biological Factors**: This includes genetics, brain chemistry, hormones, and overall physical health.

- **Psychological Factors**: Personal beliefs, emotions, thought patterns, and past experiences all impact mental health.

- **Social Factors**: Relationships, cultural background, socioeconomic status, and life events also contribute to mental well-being.

This holistic approach enables psychiatrists to consider a wide array of influences when assessing and treating a patient.

Key Roles of Psychiatry in Mental Health Care

1. Diagnosing Mental Health Conditions

One of the primary roles of psychiatry is to diagnose mental health conditions. This involves:

- **Comprehensive Assessments**: Psychiatrists use a combination of interviews, psychological tests, and physical exams to assess symptoms.

- **DSM-5 Criteria**: Psychiatrists often rely on the DSM-5 (Diagnostic and Statistical Manual of Mental Disorders) to categorize mental health conditions accurately.

- **Differential Diagnosis**: Sometimes, symptoms overlap between disorders, or physical conditions mimic psychiatric symptoms. Psychiatrists are trained to rule out other causes before making a diagnosis.

2. Developing Individualized Treatment Plans

Based on the assessment, psychiatrists create tailored treatment plans. These plans may include medication, lifestyle changes, and therapy. Each plan is unique to the individual, addressing their specific symptoms and circumstances. Effective treatment requires collaboration between psychiatrist, patient, and sometimes counselors or other healthcare providers.

3. Prescribing Medication

A unique aspect of psychiatry is the ability to prescribe medications. Medications can be instrumental in treating certain mental health conditions by correcting chemical imbalances or easing severe symptoms. However, medication is not a cure-all; it's often used in combination with counseling to achieve the best outcomes.

Types of Psychiatric Medications and Their Uses

Psychiatric medications are designed to target specific brain chemicals and neural pathways. Here are some common classes of medications and the conditions they treat:

1. Antidepressants

Antidepressants are primarily used to treat depressive disorders, but they are also effective for anxiety disorders, PTSD, and OCD. Common classes include:

- **SSRIs (Selective Serotonin Reuptake Inhibitors)**: These increase serotonin levels in the brain, which can improve mood. Examples include fluoxetine (Prozac) and sertraline (Zoloft).

- **SNRIs (Serotonin and Norepinephrine Reuptake Inhibitors)**: These target both serotonin and norepinephrine. Examples include venlafaxine (Effexor) and duloxetine (Cymbalta).

2. Antipsychotics

Antipsychotics are used for managing symptoms of schizophrenia, bipolar disorder, and sometimes severe depression. They help reduce hallucinations, delusions, and severe mood swings. Types include:

- **Typical Antipsychotics**: Older antipsychotics like haloperidol are effective but may have more side effects.

- **Atypical Antipsychotics**: Newer medications like aripiprazole (Abilify) and risperidone (Risperdal) often have fewer side effects and are widely used.

3. Mood Stabilizers

Mood stabilizers help control mood swings and are commonly prescribed for bipolar disorder. Lithium is a traditional mood stabilizer, while other medications like valproate and lamotrigine are also effective for managing bipolar symptoms.

4. Anxiolytics (Anti-Anxiety Medications)

Anxiolytics, including benzodiazepines, provide relief from acute anxiety and panic attacks. Medications such as lorazepam (Ativan) and alprazolam (Xanax) are effective for short-term use but can be habit-forming. SSRIs are also commonly used for long-term anxiety management.

5. Stimulants

Stimulants, like amphetamine (Adderall) and methylphenidate (Ritalin), are used primarily for ADHD.

They help improve focus and reduce hyperactive behavior, often enabling patients to function more effectively in daily life.

Each medication class has its benefits and potential side effects. Psychiatrists monitor these carefully, adjusting dosages and treatment plans as needed.

Combining Psychiatry and Counseling: A Holistic Approach

1. Integrated Care for Complex Conditions

While counseling addresses behavioral and emotional aspects, psychiatry can provide biological insights and medical interventions. Conditions like bipolar disorder, schizophrenia, and major depressive disorder often benefit from a combined approach:

- **Symptom Stabilization**: Medication can stabilize severe symptoms, allowing individuals to engage more fully in counseling.

- **Therapeutic Support**: Counseling helps clients work through issues that medication alone cannot address, such as trauma, relationship struggles, and coping skills.

2. Case Examples of Combined Approaches

Consider the case of Sarah, a young adult with severe anxiety and depression. Sarah's psychiatrist prescribes an SSRI to reduce her anxiety symptoms, which allows her to participate more effectively in CBT sessions with her counselor. With her anxiety under better control, Sarah is able to make meaningful progress in therapy, developing tools to manage her stress and understand her triggers.

Another example is David, a teenager with ADHD and oppositional defiant disorder. His psychiatrist prescribes a stimulant medication to help him focus, while his counselor works with him on behavior modification and social skills. The combined approach helps David improve his academic performance and build healthier relationships.

3. The Importance of Communication and Collaboration

Effective collaboration between psychiatry and counseling is essential. Both providers must communicate openly about the client's progress, potential side effects, and any emerging concerns. This communication creates a seamless approach to care, ensuring that all aspects of a client's mental health are addressed.

Common Misconceptions About Psychiatry

Despite its benefits, psychiatry often faces misunderstandings and stigma. Here are some myths and the realities behind them:

1. "Medication is a crutch and makes people weak."

- Reality: Medication can be life-saving and essential for some individuals. Far from being a "crutch," it provides stability, allowing people to engage fully in their lives.

2. "Psychiatric diagnoses are labels that limit people."

- Reality: A diagnosis is simply a tool for understanding and treating symptoms. It helps guide effective

treatment and can provide relief and clarity for
patients.

3. "Once you start medication, you're on it for life."

- Reality: Many people use medication temporarily. For
  others, long-term medication is necessary to manage
  chronic conditions, but this decision is made on a
  case-by-case basis and in collaboration with the
  patient.

Advancements in Psychiatry and Future Directions

Psychiatry continues to evolve, with research paving the
way for new treatments and approaches. Some exciting
advancements include:

1. Genetic Testing and Personalized Medicine

Pharmacogenomic testing allows psychiatrists to identify how patients may respond to specific medications based on their genetic makeup. This personalized approach can reduce trial and error in finding the right medication and may improve outcomes.

2. Neuromodulation Techniques

Innovations like Transcranial Magnetic Stimulation (TMS) and Deep Brain Stimulation (DBS) offer non-invasive options for treatment-resistant depression and other severe conditions, showing promising results.

3. Psychedelic-Assisted Therapy

Research into psychedelics, such as psilocybin and MDMA, suggests these substances can be effective when used under medical supervision for certain mental health

conditions, like PTSD and severe depression. Clinical trials
are ongoing, but initial results are encouraging.

Conclusion: The Value of Psychiatry in Mental Health

Psychiatry plays a critical role in the mental health field,
offering unique tools and expertise that complement
counseling. Through medication, in-depth diagnostics, and
evidence-based treatment plans, psychiatry can provide
stability and relief that enables individuals to participate
more fully in their healing journey.

In the next chapter, we'll explore how lifestyle changes and
holistic approaches can further support mental health,
creating a comprehensive and balanced approach to well-
being. By understanding and embracing all the tools

available, individuals can cultivate resilience and live more

fully.

Chapter 4: Lifestyle Factors and Holistic Approaches to Mental Health

Introduction to Lifestyle and Mental Health

Lifestyle choices profoundly influence mental health, and in recent years, the medical and mental health communities have increasingly recognized the importance of holistic approaches. These approaches, which consider physical, emotional, and social factors, align with the body's natural processes to create a foundation for mental wellness. In this chapter, we'll examine the role of nutrition, physical activity, sleep, and mindfulness, looking at how each can impact mood, reduce stress, and promote long-term resilience.

This holistic perspective can complement and sometimes even enhance traditional therapies, providing individuals with tools to boost their mental health outside of clinical settings. By prioritizing these lifestyle factors, individuals can empower themselves to actively participate in their mental health journey.

Nutrition and Mental Health

The Gut-Brain Connection

Scientific research increasingly supports the idea that gut health and brain health are closely interconnected. Known as the "gut-brain axis," this connection reveals how gut microbiota (the community of bacteria in the digestive system) impact brain function. The gut is sometimes referred to as the "second brain" due to its influence on neurotransmitters and mental processes. Here's how nutrition contributes to mental wellness:

- **Serotonin Production**: Around 90% of the body's serotonin—a neurotransmitter essential for mood regulation—is produced in the gut.

- **Inflammation and Mental Health**: Diets high in processed foods and sugars can increase inflammation, which has been linked to depression and anxiety.

- **Vitamins and Nutrients**: Nutrients such as Omega-3 fatty acids, B vitamins, and amino acids are essential for brain health and neurotransmitter production.

Dietary Tips for Mental Health

A balanced diet, rich in whole foods, can help stabilize mood, reduce anxiety, and promote mental clarity. Here are some evidence-based dietary recommendations:

- **Eat Whole Foods**: Prioritize vegetables, fruits, lean proteins, and whole grains to ensure balanced blood sugar and nutrient intake.

- **Include Omega-3 Fatty Acids**: Found in fish, flaxseeds, and walnuts, Omega-3s have been shown to reduce symptoms of depression.

- **Limit Processed Foods and Sugars**: These foods can cause spikes in blood sugar, leading to mood swings, fatigue, and increased inflammation.

- **Stay Hydrated**: Dehydration can impact cognitive performance and mood, so drinking plenty of water is essential.

Example Diet Plan

A sample day of balanced eating for mental wellness might include:

- **Breakfast**: Greek yogurt with berries, chia seeds, and a handful of nuts.

- **Lunch**: Grilled salmon with a quinoa salad featuring leafy greens, avocado, and a variety of colorful vegetables.

- **Dinner**: Stir-fried tofu or chicken with mixed vegetables over brown rice.

- **Snacks**: A piece of fruit, handful of almonds, or whole-grain crackers with hummus.

Physical Activity and Its Impact on Mental Health

The Science Behind Exercise and Mood

Exercise triggers the release of endorphins—chemicals in the brain that act as natural painkillers and mood elevators. It also stimulates neurotransmitters like serotonin and dopamine, which play critical roles in regulating mood, motivation, and happiness. Physical activity can be a powerful antidote to stress, anxiety, and even mild depression.

- **Reduction of Stress Hormones**: Exercise reduces levels of cortisol and adrenaline, which helps manage stress levels.

- **Improved Sleep**: Regular physical activity promotes better sleep quality, which in turn enhances mood and cognitive function.

- **Increased Resilience**: People who exercise regularly tend to feel more resilient and able to cope with challenges.

Types of Exercise for Mental Health

Different types of physical activity can have unique benefits for mental health:

- **Aerobic Exercise**: Activities like walking, running, and cycling increase heart rate and oxygen flow, promoting a sense of calm and reducing anxiety.

- **Strength Training**: Building physical strength can increase self-esteem and reduce symptoms of depression, particularly in young adults.

- **Yoga and Pilates**: These activities combine physical movement with breathing exercises, fostering mindfulness and reducing stress.

- **Outdoor Activities**: Time spent in nature, such as hiking or biking outdoors, can improve mood and reduce mental fatigue.

Suggested Routine

For mental health benefits, aim for at least 150 minutes of moderate exercise each week, or 30 minutes five times per week. Start with activities you enjoy, and focus on making exercise a sustainable part of your lifestyle rather than a chore.

The Critical Role of Sleep in Mental Wellness

The Science of Sleep and the Brain

Sleep is crucial for brain function, emotional regulation, and cognitive performance. Lack of sleep can impair memory, reduce concentration, and lead to irritability and anxiety. Here's how sleep affects mental health:

- **Emotional Regulation**: Sleep helps the brain process emotions, reducing reactivity to stress and improving mood stability.

- **Memory Consolidation**: During sleep, the brain consolidates memories, which is essential for learning and emotional processing.

- **Hormonal Balance**: Sleep regulates hormones that impact mood, such as cortisol and melatonin.

Tips for Better Sleep Hygiene

Good sleep hygiene promotes restful sleep and overall mental well-being:

- **Maintain a Regular Sleep Schedule**: Going to bed and waking up at the same time each day supports the body's internal clock.

- **Create a Calming Bedtime Routine**: Reading, meditating, or listening to soothing music before bed can signal the body to wind down.

- **Limit Screen Time**: Avoid screens at least one hour before bedtime, as blue light from devices can disrupt melatonin production.

- **Avoid Stimulants**: Caffeine and nicotine can interfere with sleep; try to limit these, especially in the afternoon and evening.

Managing Sleep Disorders

For those who struggle with sleep disorders like insomnia or sleep apnea, consulting with a healthcare provider is essential. Treatment options might include cognitive behavioral therapy for insomnia (CBT-I), sleep apnea treatments, or lifestyle adjustments.

Mindfulness and Stress Management

Understanding Mindfulness

Mindfulness is the practice of staying present in the moment and observing thoughts and emotions without judgment. This practice can reduce stress, improve mood, and enhance self-awareness. In mental health, mindfulness is often used to address anxiety, depression, and stress by fostering a sense of inner calm and control.

Benefits of Mindfulness for Mental Health

- **Stress Reduction**: Mindfulness can reduce cortisol levels, decreasing overall stress.

- **Increased Emotional Awareness**: Mindfulness helps individuals recognize and understand their emotions, enabling healthier responses.

- **Improved Focus**: Practicing mindfulness can enhance concentration and reduce symptoms of attention disorders.

Techniques for Practicing Mindfulness

Incorporating mindfulness doesn't have to be complicated. Here are some techniques that can be done almost anywhere:

- **Breathing Exercises**: Deep breathing, such as box breathing (inhaling for four counts, holding for four, exhaling for four), can calm the nervous system.

- **Body Scans**: This practice involves mentally scanning the body from head to toe, noting sensations and tension areas.

- **Guided Meditation**: Using apps or audio guides, individuals can practice mindfulness in sessions ranging from 5 to 30 minutes.

- **Mindful Activities**: Everyday tasks like eating, walking, or washing dishes can become opportunities for mindfulness by focusing on each sensation and movement.

Integrating Holistic Approaches into Daily Life

Creating a Personalized Wellness Routine

The best holistic routines are those that are sustainable and enjoyable. Individuals should select activities that align with their values, schedule, and lifestyle. Here's a sample weekly routine that combines the elements of nutrition, exercise, sleep, and mindfulness:

- **Monday**: Start the day with a short meditation, focus on a balanced diet, and go for a brisk walk in the evening.

- **Wednesday**: Prepare a nutritious dinner high in Omega-3s, practice mindfulness through deep breathing, and go to bed at a consistent time.

- **Friday**: Join a yoga or Pilates class to combine physical movement with mindfulness.

- **Weekend**: Spend time outdoors to refresh the mind and connect with nature, practice gratitude journaling in the evening.

Building Resilience and Self-Care

Self-care is a proactive approach to mental health, giving individuals the energy and resilience needed to cope with life's demands. By integrating these holistic practices, individuals build an internal foundation that strengthens over time.

Conclusion: The Power of Holistic Approaches in Mental Health

Lifestyle factors are often overlooked in mental health care, but as this chapter demonstrates, they play an essential role in promoting mental wellness. A commitment to balanced nutrition, regular physical activity, sufficient sleep, and mindfulness can greatly enhance one's ability to manage stress, improve mood, and increase resilience.

In the following chapters, we will continue to explore additional support systems and coping mechanisms that contribute to mental well-being, helping readers develop a comprehensive, well-rounded approach to mental health care.

Chapter 5: Building Strong Support Systems: The Role of Relationships in Mental Health

Introduction to Social Support and Mental Health

Human beings are inherently social creatures. While everyone's need for social connection may vary, positive relationships are crucial for mental well-being. From family and friends to community networks and professional support, each social connection can serve as a buffer against life's challenges, helping individuals cope more effectively with stress, anxiety, and even symptoms of mental illness. Strong support systems empower people to feel understood, valued, and less isolated in times of need, making relationships foundational to a healthy life.

In this chapter, we'll discuss the different types of relationships that contribute to mental health, the qualities that make relationships beneficial, and ways to cultivate support systems. For many, mental health struggles can lead to isolation, but reaching out to build and strengthen connections can provide much-needed support and healing.

Understanding the Types of Supportive Relationships

Family Support

Family is often the first place where we experience love, acceptance, and connection. Healthy family relationships can offer a sense of stability and understanding, forming a strong foundation for mental resilience. While every family is different, having a stable family connection can positively impact self-esteem and confidence, making it easier to face life's challenges. However, family relationships can sometimes be complex and require patience, boundaries, and effective communication to nurture supportive dynamics.

Friendships

Friends play a unique role in providing emotional support, companionship, and encouragement. Friendships give individuals the freedom to express themselves without judgment, providing a safe space for discussing worries, insecurities, and dreams. Friends can also help in grounding us, providing perspective during difficult times, and offering humor and joy in daily life. Friendships, therefore, serve as a form of "chosen family," offering mutual respect and understanding.

Romantic Relationships

Romantic partners can offer an essential level of intimacy, trust, and support. A healthy romantic relationship provides a safe haven where individuals can be vulnerable, share their goals, and receive emotional support. In the context of mental health, partners can be a source of encouragement, motivation, and security. However, this also requires open communication, respect for boundaries, and an understanding of each other's needs.

Community and Spiritual Connections

Community can come in many forms: neighborhoods, faith-based organizations, support groups, or clubs. These connections offer a sense of belonging and purpose beyond individual relationships. Faith-based communities, in particular, can provide spiritual guidance and support, reminding individuals of something larger than themselves and instilling a sense of hope and purpose. For many, spirituality provides a profound sense of comfort and resilience.

Professional Support Networks

Mental health professionals, such as therapists, counselors, and support group facilitators, can offer structured, evidence-based support that's essential in times of mental health struggles. Professionals provide a safe environment for exploring emotions, gaining new insights, and developing coping skills. While friends and family are critical, professional support is unique in its focus on mental health and healing.

The Benefits of Strong Support Systems

Emotional Stability

Having people who provide unconditional support can significantly impact one's emotional stability. A stable support system can reduce feelings of loneliness, increase self-esteem, and offer reassurance during challenging times.

- **Increased Resilience**: People with strong support systems are generally more resilient to stress and trauma. They are less likely to feel overwhelmed by setbacks and better able to recover from hardships.

- **Sense of Belonging**: Knowing you are part of a group or relationship provides a feeling of belonging, which is key to combating isolation and depression.

- **Encouragement and Motivation**: Supportive relationships offer motivation to pursue personal goals, maintain healthy habits, and seek professional help when needed.

Practical Assistance

In times of crisis, support systems provide more than just emotional comfort. Family, friends, and community members can offer practical assistance, such as childcare, help with errands, or financial support, which can relieve stress and allow individuals to focus on their mental health needs.

Constructive Feedback

Supportive relationships can provide constructive feedback, helping individuals gain perspective and grow. Honest conversations with loved ones can help people see different viewpoints, recognize areas for improvement, and build a stronger sense of self-awareness.

How to Build and Strengthen Support Systems

Nurturing Existing Relationships

Building a support system doesn't always mean creating new connections; it can also involve strengthening bonds with existing family, friends, or colleagues. Here are ways to deepen these relationships:

- **Active Listening**: When engaging with others, practice active listening by giving them your full attention. Show empathy, validate their feelings, and refrain from offering unsolicited advice.

- **Expressing Appreciation**: Show gratitude by regularly acknowledging the positive things loved ones bring to your life. A simple "thank you" can strengthen bonds and encourage reciprocation.

- **Being Vulnerable**: Share your thoughts, feelings, and struggles openly with trusted individuals. Vulnerability invites others to connect more deeply, creating a safe space for mutual support.

- **Consistent Communication**: Check in with your loved ones regularly, even during good times. Maintaining consistent contact fosters trust and reliability.

Expanding Your Circle

If you feel your current support system isn't sufficient, consider expanding your circle to include others who share your interests and values. Here are some strategies:

- **Join Groups or Clubs**: Look for community organizations, clubs, or hobby groups that align with your interests. This could include sports teams, volunteer organizations, or book clubs.

- **Attend Faith-Based Groups**: For those with a religious or spiritual background, faith communities offer connection, guidance, and support.

- **Connect Online**: While in-person connections are ideal, online communities can also provide meaningful support. There are numerous forums, groups, and resources available for those looking to connect virtually.

Seeking Professional Support

If you struggle to build a support system or need specialized help, mental health professionals provide a safe space for personal growth. Counseling and support groups can equip individuals with coping strategies and a non-judgmental environment to process their feelings.

Managing Challenging Relationships

While positive relationships are essential for mental health, not all relationships are beneficial. Toxic relationships—those characterized by manipulation, criticism, or control—can have a detrimental effect on mental well-being. Managing these relationships requires setting healthy boundaries and, in some cases, minimizing or ending contact. Here are some ways to manage challenging dynamics:

- **Setting Boundaries**: Establish clear boundaries regarding what is acceptable behavior. This can mean limiting conversations about certain topics, designating personal time, or asserting your needs.

- **Communicating Assertively**: Use "I" statements to express feelings without placing blame. For example, "I feel overwhelmed when discussions become negative, so I'd like to focus on positive topics."

- **Knowing When to Distance**: If a relationship consistently harms your mental health, it may be best to step back or create distance. This could mean interacting less frequently or limiting the depth of engagement.

- **Seeking Support for Difficult Decisions**: Ending or distancing from a relationship is often challenging.

Seek guidance from a counselor, support group, or trusted friend to process these decisions.

Maintaining and Strengthening Your Support System

Investing in Relationships

Building a support system isn't a one-time task; it requires consistent effort and attention. Prioritize time for the people who support you and make an effort to show up for them as well.

Reaching Out During Difficult Times

In moments of mental health crises, reach out to your support network. If you feel hesitant to share your struggles, remind yourself that loved ones care and want to be there for you. Support systems are often strengthened through openness and vulnerability, especially during challenging times.

Regularly Evaluating Your Relationships

As you grow, it's natural for your relationships to evolve. Regularly assess the dynamics of your relationships and make changes to ensure they support your mental health goals. This may mean strengthening certain bonds or letting go of relationships that no longer serve you.

Conclusion: The Power of Connection in Mental Health

A strong support system is invaluable for mental well-being. Meaningful relationships provide love, understanding, and guidance, which can buffer against stress and promote resilience. By nurturing relationships, setting healthy boundaries, and reaching out during difficult times, individuals can create a support network that enhances both mental and emotional health.

In the next chapter, we'll explore therapeutic interventions that complement these supportive relationships, offering structured ways to address mental health challenges and build emotional resilience.

Chapter 6: Therapeutic Interventions and Their Transformative Power

Introduction to Therapeutic Interventions in Mental Health

Therapeutic interventions form the backbone of mental health treatment. While medications can play a role in symptom management, therapy addresses the root causes of mental health issues and provides strategies for long-term resilience. Working with a therapist offers individuals a safe space to explore their thoughts, feelings, and behaviors and develop coping mechanisms to handle life's challenges. Therapy, in its various forms, allows people to make profound changes in their perspectives, relationships, and self-awareness.

In this chapter, we will look at the most common types of therapy, the principles behind them, and how they work to support emotional and psychological well-being. We'll also provide guidance on selecting the right therapeutic approach for your unique situation.

The Foundation of Psychotherapy: Understanding the Basics

The Purpose of Therapy

Therapy, at its core, provides a supportive, non-judgmental environment where individuals can gain insight into their thoughts, emotions, and behaviors. By examining life experiences, relationships, and personal challenges, therapy helps individuals uncover patterns, develop healthier coping strategies, and achieve a sense of balance.

Therapists use various therapeutic techniques, drawing from psychological theories and empirical research, to guide clients toward personal growth. The goal of therapy isn't just to alleviate symptoms; it's to empower individuals with the tools they need to live fulfilling lives, improve relationships, and enhance self-esteem.

The Therapeutic Relationship

One of the most important components of successful therapy is the therapeutic relationship, or the bond between therapist and client. A strong therapeutic alliance is built on trust, empathy, and open communication, and it allows clients to feel safe in sharing their vulnerabilities. The therapeutic relationship itself can be healing, as it provides a model for healthy, supportive relationships outside the therapy room.

Cognitive Behavioral Therapy (CBT): Changing Thoughts and Behaviors

The Basics of CBT

Cognitive Behavioral Therapy (CBT) is one of the most widely used and researched forms of therapy. It is based on the principle that our thoughts, emotions, and behaviors are interconnected. By changing negative thought patterns, individuals can positively affect their emotions and actions, leading to improved mental health.

CBT focuses on identifying and challenging "cognitive distortions" – irrational thoughts that fuel negative emotions, such as catastrophizing, black-and-white thinking, or personalizing events. Therapists use various techniques to help clients reframe these thoughts and practice new, healthier ways of thinking and responding.

Techniques in CBT

- **Thought Records**: Clients record distressing situations, the thoughts associated with those situations, and alternative, balanced thoughts. This practice helps them recognize and challenge cognitive distortions in real time.

- **Exposure Therapy**: This technique is often used for anxiety and involves gradually exposing clients to the situations or objects that cause them fear, allowing them to face their anxieties in a controlled environment.

- **Behavioral Activation**: Often used for depression, this technique encourages clients to engage in positive activities that provide a sense of accomplishment or pleasure, thereby breaking the cycle of avoidance and low mood.

Effectiveness of CBT

CBT has been shown to be highly effective for a range of mental health issues, including depression, anxiety, PTSD, and eating disorders. Because it is skill-based and focused on specific, measurable goals, CBT can often provide noticeable results within a few months.

Dialectical Behavior Therapy (DBT): Balancing Acceptance and Change

The Basics of DBT

Originally developed for individuals with borderline personality disorder, Dialectical Behavior Therapy (DBT) has since been adapted to help people with various emotional regulation issues, including mood disorders, self-harm behaviors, and suicidal ideation. DBT combines principles from CBT with mindfulness practices, helping individuals manage intense emotions without acting impulsively.

Core Skills in DBT

- **Mindfulness**: DBT teaches clients to be fully present in the moment, enhancing awareness of their thoughts, feelings, and surroundings. This skill helps individuals become more in control of their emotional responses.

- **Distress Tolerance**: This skill helps clients cope with crises in a healthy way, without resorting to self-destructive behaviors. Techniques include grounding exercises, distraction, and self-soothing practices.

- **Emotional Regulation**: Clients learn strategies for managing their emotional responses, reducing vulnerability to intense emotional swings, and identifying positive activities that stabilize their mood.

- **Interpersonal Effectiveness**: DBT focuses on building strong, healthy relationships. It teaches clients to assertively communicate their needs, set boundaries, and handle conflict in constructive ways.

Effectiveness of DBT

DBT is especially effective for individuals struggling with emotional dysregulation and impulsive behaviors. Research shows that DBT can reduce suicidal behavior, self-harm, and emotional instability, empowering clients to handle distress in healthy ways.

Psychodynamic Therapy: Uncovering the Subconscious Mind

The Basics of Psychodynamic Therapy

Psychodynamic therapy is rooted in the work of Sigmund Freud and later psychoanalysts. This approach explores how unconscious thoughts and feelings, often rooted in childhood experiences, influence present-day behaviors. The goal is to increase self-awareness and understanding of how past experiences shape current patterns and relationships.

Free Association and Dream Analysis

- **Free Association**: Clients are encouraged to speak freely about whatever comes to mind. This helps uncover unconscious thoughts and emotions, providing insight into the root causes of distress.

- **Dream Analysis**: Some psychodynamic therapists analyze dreams as a way to understand unresolved conflicts or hidden fears that may be affecting the individual's mental health.

Effectiveness of Psychodynamic Therapy

Though it may take longer than CBT or DBT, psychodynamic therapy can be transformative, offering deep insights that lead to long-term changes. It is particularly effective for individuals seeking to understand relationship issues, self-esteem challenges, or repetitive patterns of behavior.

Humanistic and Person-Centered Therapy: Emphasizing Self-Growth and Empathy

The Basics of Humanistic Therapy

Humanistic therapy, also known as person-centered therapy, was developed by Carl Rogers. It focuses on helping clients reach their full potential by emphasizing self-acceptance, empathy, and personal growth. The therapist provides unconditional positive regard, creating a supportive environment in which clients feel free to explore their thoughts and emotions.

Core Principles

- **Unconditional Positive Regard**: The therapist shows non-judgmental acceptance and empathy, allowing clients to feel valued and understood.

- **Self-Actualization**: The goal is to help clients realize their full potential, leading to self-fulfillment and a stronger sense of identity.

- **Client Autonomy**: Humanistic therapists believe that clients know themselves best and should lead their own healing journey. The therapist's role is to guide, rather than direct.

Effectiveness of Humanistic Therapy

Humanistic therapy is beneficial for individuals seeking self-improvement, increased self-esteem, and personal growth. It is often used for general mental wellness rather than specific mental health conditions, though it can be powerful in combination with other therapeutic approaches.

Trauma-Focused Therapies: Healing from Past Wounds

Understanding Trauma Therapy

Trauma-focused therapy is designed to help individuals process and recover from traumatic experiences. This approach acknowledges that trauma can have long-lasting effects on the brain and body, leading to issues like PTSD, anxiety, depression, and emotional dysregulation.

Types of Trauma Therapies

- **Eye Movement Desensitization and Reprocessing (EMDR)**: EMDR uses guided eye movements to help clients process traumatic memories and reduce their emotional impact.

- **Trauma-Focused CBT**: This therapy combines elements of CBT with trauma-focused techniques, helping individuals confront and process traumatic memories in a safe, supportive environment.

- **Somatic Experiencing**: This therapy focuses on releasing trauma stored in the body, helping clients reconnect with their physical sensations to heal emotional wounds.

Effectiveness of Trauma Therapies

Trauma-focused therapies have been shown to reduce symptoms of PTSD, anxiety, and other trauma-related conditions. They are crucial for individuals who feel "stuck" in the aftermath of trauma, providing structured techniques for healing.

Choosing the Right Therapy for Your Needs

Assessing Personal Goals

Choosing the right therapy begins with understanding your personal goals and the challenges you want to address. Each therapeutic approach offers unique benefits, so it's essential to consider which approach aligns best with your needs.

Consulting with a Mental Health Professional

Mental health professionals can provide valuable guidance in selecting a therapy that matches your specific concerns. Many therapists offer an initial consultation to discuss treatment goals, helping you decide if their approach is a good fit.

Combining Therapies

In many cases, combining therapies—such as using CBT with trauma-focused methods—can provide a more comprehensive approach to treatment. Working with a therapist who integrates multiple approaches can be beneficial for complex mental health needs.

Conclusion: Embracing the Transformative Power of Therapy

Therapy can transform lives by offering new perspectives, skills, and insights that foster resilience and healing. By understanding the wide range of therapeutic options available, individuals can feel empowered to choose an approach that aligns with their unique needs and goals.

With the guidance of skilled professionals, therapy can

provide a path to personal growth, inner peace, and

emotional freedom.

Chapter 7: The Role of Medication in Mental Health Treatment

Introduction: Understanding Medication in Mental Health Care

Mental health treatment often involves a combination of therapeutic approaches, with medication serving as a critical tool for managing symptoms and enhancing the effectiveness of therapy. While therapy addresses the root causes of mental health issues, medication can help stabilize symptoms, providing a foundation for individuals to engage fully in the therapeutic process. For some, medication may be a short-term support; for others, it may become a long-term part of managing a chronic condition.

In this chapter, we'll delve into the types of psychiatric medications, discuss how they work, and outline what patients should consider before beginning any medication regimen. We'll also emphasize the importance of ongoing communication with healthcare providers to adjust and optimize medication plans for each unique individual.

The Purpose and Scope of Psychiatric Medication

Why Medication Matters in Mental Health

Medications can be life-changing for those struggling with mental health conditions that impact mood, perception, concentration, and behavior. They can play a vital role in stabilizing brain chemistry, allowing individuals to function more effectively and experience an improved quality of life.

While medication does not "cure" mental health conditions, it can reduce or alleviate symptoms to a manageable level, enabling people to engage more fully in other aspects of their treatment, such as therapy, lifestyle adjustments, and self-care practices.

When Medication is Considered

Medication may be recommended when:

- Symptoms are severe or persistent and interfere significantly with daily life.

- Other forms of treatment, such as therapy, have not provided sufficient relief on their own.

- Individuals have biological predispositions or conditions that respond well to medication, such as bipolar disorder, schizophrenia, or major depressive disorder.

- The individual experiences acute distress, such as intense anxiety or suicidal thoughts, where medication can provide more immediate relief.

Integrating Medication with Therapy

Medication and therapy are often more effective when used together. While medication addresses symptoms, therapy can help individuals understand and work through underlying issues. Combining the two can improve adherence to treatment plans, support long-term wellness, and reduce the likelihood of relapse.

Types of Psychiatric Medications and Their Functions

Antidepressants

- **Purpose**: Primarily used to treat depression, anxiety disorders, and some chronic pain conditions.

- **Types**: The main classes include SSRIs (Selective Serotonin Reuptake Inhibitors), SNRIs (Serotonin and Norepinephrine Reuptake Inhibitors), and tricyclic antidepressants.

- **How They Work**: Antidepressants balance neurotransmitters in the brain, such as serotonin and norepinephrine, which influence mood and emotion.

Anti-Anxiety Medications

- **Purpose**: These medications help reduce symptoms of anxiety disorders, panic attacks, and certain phobias.

- **Types**: Commonly prescribed anti-anxiety medications include benzodiazepines and certain antidepressants.

- **How They Work**: Anti-anxiety medications work by calming the central nervous system, often by enhancing the effects of GABA (gamma-aminobutyric acid), a neurotransmitter associated with relaxation and stress reduction.

Mood Stabilizers

- **Purpose**: Used primarily for bipolar disorder and mood swings associated with other mental health conditions.

- **Types**: Lithium, anticonvulsants, and certain antipsychotics can act as mood stabilizers.

- **How They Work**: Mood stabilizers help regulate extreme mood shifts by influencing brain chemicals associated with mood control, like serotonin and dopamine.

Antipsychotics

- **Purpose**: Primarily prescribed for schizophrenia, bipolar disorder, and severe depression.

- **Types**: There are typical (first-generation) and atypical (second-generation) antipsychotics, with atypical ones being more commonly used today due to fewer side effects.

- **How They Work**: These medications alter the effects of dopamine and, to a lesser extent, serotonin in the brain, reducing symptoms like hallucinations, delusions, and disorganized thinking.

Stimulants

- **Purpose**: Mostly used for attention-deficit/hyperactivity disorder (ADHD).

- **Types**: Common stimulants include amphetamine and methylphenidate.

- **How They Work**: Stimulants increase the levels of dopamine and norepinephrine in the brain, improving focus, attention, and impulse control in people with ADHD.

Considerations When Starting Medication

Evaluating Benefits vs. Risks

Before starting medication, it's crucial to weigh the potential benefits against the risks, which include possible side effects. For many, the benefits can vastly outweigh the risks, especially when symptoms are debilitating. However, understanding potential side effects, such as fatigue, weight gain, or changes in mood, helps individuals make informed decisions.

Importance of Personalized Care

Each person's response to medication can differ based on factors like genetics, overall health, and lifestyle. Personalized care, including genetic testing in some cases, can help predict which medications might be most effective and which dosages are likely to be optimal. This personalized approach reduces trial and error, supporting a smoother path to stability.

Setting Realistic Expectations

While some medications can produce relatively quick improvements, others, like antidepressants, may take weeks before their full effects are felt. Understanding the timeline and gradual nature of medication's impact can help individuals stay motivated and avoid prematurely discontinuing treatment.

The Role of Monitoring and Adjustments

Ongoing Communication with Healthcare Providers

Regular check-ins with a healthcare provider are essential to assess how well the medication is working and address any side effects. Adjustments in dosage, a change in medication, or additional support can make a significant difference in treatment success.

The Process of Titration

Titration refers to the careful adjustment of medication doses. In many cases, healthcare providers start with a low dose and gradually increase it to find the minimum effective dose that controls symptoms with the least side effects. This gradual approach reduces the likelihood of adverse reactions and helps individuals adapt more comfortably.

Handling Side Effects

Side effects can sometimes be a barrier to medication adherence. In these cases, healthcare providers can suggest strategies to manage or mitigate side effects, adjust the dosage, or even switch to a different medication if necessary.

The Debate Surrounding Psychiatric Medication

Addressing Stigma

Despite the prevalence of mental health issues, stigma around psychiatric medication persists. Many people feel hesitant to take medication due to fears of dependency, side effects, or judgment from others. Addressing these concerns with facts and reducing stigma can help individuals feel more comfortable with medication as a legitimate form of treatment.

The Role of Medication in Modern Psychiatry

Some argue that medication is overprescribed or that society is overly reliant on pharmaceutical solutions. However, when used judiciously and as part of a comprehensive treatment plan, medication can be an invaluable resource. While medication is not a "cure," it plays a crucial role in stabilizing symptoms, particularly in severe cases where symptoms are overwhelming or life-threatening.

Alternative and Complementary Approaches

Medication is not the only approach to managing mental health symptoms. Complementary therapies, such as exercise, mindfulness, diet adjustments, and certain supplements, can enhance the effects of medication and contribute to overall wellness. In many cases, these alternatives can reduce the need for higher doses of medication, creating a balanced approach to mental health care.

Ending Medication: When and How to Discontinue

Signs That It May Be Time to Reduce or Stop Medication

For some individuals, long-term medication may be unnecessary, and symptoms can be managed through therapy and lifestyle changes. Signs that it may be appropriate to reduce or stop medication include sustained symptom remission, successful therapy outcomes, and improved coping skills.

The Importance of Tapering

Discontinuing medication abruptly can lead to withdrawal symptoms or a return of symptoms. Tapering off medication under a healthcare provider's guidance is essential to prevent these effects and ensure a smoother transition. A gradual reduction in dosage allows the brain to adjust and minimizes potential side effects.

The Potential for Relapse

Even after stopping medication, it's essential to monitor for any signs of relapse and remain connected with mental health support. Having a proactive plan in place and maintaining a relationship with a therapist or healthcare provider can provide peace of mind and ensure prompt support if symptoms reemerge.

Conclusion: Medication as a Tool in Holistic Mental Health Care

Medication is a powerful tool in the mental health treatment toolkit, capable of transforming lives when used thoughtfully and as part of a comprehensive care plan. While not the only answer, it is often the support that individuals need to break free from debilitating symptoms, regain control, and pursue meaningful growth.

Whether you are considering medication for the first time, currently on a medication regimen, or exploring alternative options, the goal remains the same: to achieve a state of balance, resilience, and well-being that supports your highest potential. By integrating medication, therapy, and self-care, individuals can create a robust approach to mental health that empowers them to live with purpose and hope.

In the next chapter, we'll explore the broader role of lifestyle changes and self-care in supporting mental health.

Chapter 8: The Power of Self-Care and Lifestyle Changes in Mental Health

Introduction: Embracing Self-Care as a Foundation for Mental Health

Self-care has often been relegated to the realm of luxuries or "extras," yet the reality is that self-care practices are foundational to achieving and sustaining mental health. Our daily habits, choices, and the ways we respond to stressors play a crucial role in influencing our emotional well-being and resilience. For individuals struggling with mental health conditions, self-care can be a transformative addition to traditional treatments like therapy and medication, often enhancing their effectiveness.

This chapter will outline key areas of self-care, providing practical strategies for integrating these practices into your life to support your mental and emotional health.

Physical Health and Its Connection to Mental Well-being

The Influence of Physical Health on Mental State

The link between physical health and mental health is profound. Physical activity, diet, and sleep are not only essential for our bodies but also have direct impacts on how we feel, think, and interact with the world. Physical self-care is more than just about being "fit" — it's about nurturing the body in a way that promotes energy, clarity, and resilience.

Exercise and Mental Health

- **Benefits**: Exercise increases the production of neurotransmitters like serotonin, dopamine, and endorphins, all of which are associated with mood regulation and stress relief. Regular physical activity has been shown to reduce symptoms of depression, anxiety, and even chronic pain.

- **Types of Exercise**: While high-intensity workouts offer significant benefits, even low-impact exercises like walking, yoga, or stretching can reduce stress and promote mental clarity. The key is consistency and finding activities that feel enjoyable and sustainable.

- **Creating a Routine**: Aim for at least 30 minutes of moderate physical activity most days of the week. Break it down into smaller intervals if needed; what matters most is building a routine that you can maintain.

Nutrition and Brain Health

- **Diet and Mood**: Diet influences brain function, and certain nutrients are essential for maintaining mental health. Omega-3 fatty acids, B vitamins, and antioxidants are known to support cognitive function and mood regulation.

- **Blood Sugar Balance**: Blood sugar fluctuations can impact energy and mood. Eating balanced meals with proteins, healthy fats, and complex carbohydrates helps stabilize blood sugar, reducing irritability and fatigue.

- **Hydration**: Dehydration is often overlooked but can have an immediate impact on mental clarity, energy, and mood. Drinking enough water throughout the day is an essential aspect of self-care.

The Importance of Sleep

- **Sleep and Mental Health**: Sleep is critical for emotional regulation, memory processing, and overall cognitive function. Poor sleep can exacerbate symptoms of anxiety and depression, while adequate rest can enhance resilience and clarity.

- **Sleep Hygiene**: Good sleep hygiene includes maintaining a regular sleep schedule, creating a relaxing bedtime routine, and limiting stimulants like caffeine and screen time before bed.

- **Addressing Sleep Issues**: If sleep issues persist, consider speaking with a healthcare provider. They can help identify underlying issues, such as sleep disorders or stress-related insomnia, and suggest effective treatments.

Emotional Self-Care: Cultivating Inner Peace and Resilience

Recognizing and Validating Emotions

Emotional self-care begins with acknowledging and validating your emotions. This means allowing yourself to feel without judgment, understanding that emotions are natural responses to life's challenges and joys.

Practices for Emotional Self-Care

- **Mindfulness and Meditation**: These practices teach us to observe thoughts and feelings without becoming overwhelmed by them. Daily mindfulness or meditation, even for a few minutes, can increase emotional resilience and reduce stress.

- **Journaling**: Writing down thoughts and feelings is a powerful tool for processing emotions, gaining insights, and identifying recurring patterns. Journaling can be particularly helpful for those dealing with overwhelming emotions or complex mental health challenges.

- **Breathwork and Relaxation Techniques**: Deep breathing, progressive muscle relaxation, and visualization exercises can help calm the mind and reduce anxiety. Practicing these techniques regularly can enhance emotional control, especially in high-stress situations.

Setting Healthy Boundaries

Boundaries are essential for protecting emotional well-being. Learning to say "no," respecting your own limits, and ensuring that relationships are mutually respectful and supportive all contribute to emotional health.

Social Self-Care: Nurturing Supportive Relationships

The Impact of Social Connections on Mental Health

Humans are inherently social beings, and strong, positive relationships are vital for mental health. Social support acts as a buffer against stress, providing perspective, comfort, and motivation when life gets tough. Conversely, isolation and loneliness can intensify symptoms of depression, anxiety, and other mental health challenges.

Building and Maintaining a Support Network

- **Family and Friends**: Strong connections with family and friends provide emotional support, companionship, and a sense of belonging. Make time to nurture these relationships through regular contact, shared activities, and open communication.

- **Peer Support and Community Groups**: Engaging in group activities or support groups can provide a safe space for discussing challenges, sharing experiences, and gaining encouragement. This can be particularly helpful for those dealing with specific mental health issues, such as grief, addiction, or trauma.

- **Setting Boundaries in Relationships**: While supportive relationships are beneficial, toxic or overly demanding relationships can drain emotional energy. Setting boundaries protects mental well-being and allows for healthier, more fulfilling connections.

The Importance of Giving Back

Helping others can boost self-esteem, foster purpose, and improve mental health. Volunteering, offering support to those in need, or contributing to a cause can cultivate gratitude and provide perspective, which can have profound effects on mental and emotional well-being.

Spiritual Self-Care: Finding Purpose and Meaning

The Role of Spirituality in Mental Health

Spirituality can provide a sense of purpose, connection, and peace, all of which are beneficial for mental health. For some, spirituality may be rooted in religious beliefs, while for others, it may involve connecting with nature, practicing gratitude, or exploring personal values and purpose.

Practices for Spiritual Self-Care

- **Prayer and Meditation**: For those who follow a religious path, prayer can be a source of comfort, guidance, and strength. Meditation, even in a secular form, can help individuals connect with a sense of inner calm and clarity.

- **Gratitude Practice**: Regularly expressing gratitude has been shown to improve mood, reduce stress, and enhance overall life satisfaction. Consider keeping a gratitude journal or setting aside time each day to reflect on things you're thankful for.

- **Connecting with Nature**: Spending time in nature can be grounding and rejuvenating. Nature can provide a sense of perspective, helping individuals to feel part of something greater than themselves.

Exploring Purpose and Values

Understanding personal values and pursuing goals that align with them can provide direction and meaning. Engaging in activities that reflect one's core values fosters resilience, as individuals feel more fulfilled and grounded even during challenging times.

Creating a Personalized Self-Care Plan

Assessing Your Self-Care Needs

Developing a self-care routine involves assessing your current needs and challenges. Consider which areas of life (physical, emotional, social, or spiritual) could benefit from additional attention and identify specific practices that resonate with you.

Setting Realistic Goals

Start with small, achievable goals. Rather than overhauling your entire routine, introduce one or two self-care practices that you can commit to consistently. Over time, these small steps build into a solid foundation for mental health.

Building Self-Care into Daily Life

Incorporate self-care practices into your daily or weekly routines. Consistency is key; a routine helps make self-care a natural and regular part of life. For example, set aside time each morning for mindfulness, or schedule regular meet-ups with friends.

Self-Care as a Dynamic Process

Self-care needs can change over time. Reevaluate your practices periodically, adjusting them to meet your evolving mental and physical health needs. Being flexible and open to change ensures that self-care remains a supportive and effective component of your mental health journey.

Conclusion: Embracing Self-Care for Long-Term Mental Health

Self-care and lifestyle adjustments are not luxuries but essential components of a healthy, balanced life. By prioritizing physical, emotional, social, and spiritual well-being, we create a resilient foundation that supports mental health through life's inevitable challenges.

In the next chapter, we'll discuss the crucial aspect of overcoming mental health stigma and advocating for compassionate, inclusive attitudes toward mental health treatment. Together, self-care and a supportive community make a profound impact on the journey to mental wellness.

Chapter 9: Breaking the Stigma: Advocating for Mental Health Awareness

Introduction: The Burden of Stigma in Mental Health

Despite advances in mental health awareness, stigma continues to be a powerful barrier preventing many individuals from seeking the help they need. Stigma breeds silence, shame, and fear, and often forces people to hide their struggles or forego treatment altogether. Stigma has both external and internal dimensions—society's judgmental attitudes, as well as individuals' self-stigmatization, wherein they internalize these negative stereotypes.

The consequences of this are far-reaching, contributing to worsening mental health conditions, social isolation, and unnecessary suffering. However, with awareness, education, and collective action, we can challenge and change these harmful attitudes. This chapter will discuss the origins of mental health stigma, the specific challenges it creates, and the importance of advocacy for a healthier, more compassionate society.

Understanding the Roots of Mental Health Stigma

Historical Perspectives on Mental Illness

Stigma has its roots in ancient misconceptions about mental illness, with historical explanations ranging from possession by spirits to moral weakness. These myths have been largely debunked, yet remnants of such beliefs continue to shape public perceptions. Over centuries, people with mental health conditions were often marginalized, institutionalized, and ostracized, fueling misunderstandings and mistrust around the topic.

Media and Its Influence

Media representations have historically reinforced stigma. From sensationalized news stories to fictional portrayals of individuals with mental health conditions as unstable or dangerous, these depictions create and perpetuate false and damaging stereotypes. Even today, some media outlets prioritize stories that exaggerate or oversimplify mental health conditions, leading to a general misrepresentation in the public eye.

Cultural Beliefs and Norms

Cultural beliefs play a significant role in shaping attitudes toward mental health. In some cultures, mental health issues may be regarded as personal failures, leading to secrecy and denial. In others, mental health may not be recognized or understood as a legitimate concern, with individuals encouraged to "just be strong" or "pray it away." These cultural attitudes create barriers to treatment, as individuals may feel their struggles are invalid or unworthy of professional support.

The Impact of Stigma on Individuals

Barrier to Seeking Help

Stigma discourages people from seeking help out of fear of judgment, discrimination, or being perceived as "weak" or "incapable." Many people avoid seeking treatment until their symptoms become severe, leading to delayed diagnoses and worsening conditions. This delay can have profound effects on one's life, impacting relationships, work, and overall quality of life.

Isolation and Shame

Stigma can also lead to self-stigmatization, where individuals internalize negative societal beliefs about mental illness. This can result in feelings of shame, isolation, and self-doubt. Self-stigma erodes self-esteem and confidence, causing people to withdraw from social interactions and hide their struggles rather than reach out for support.

Workplace and Social Discrimination

In the workplace, stigma may manifest as discriminatory practices, such as reluctance to hire, promote, or fairly compensate individuals with mental health conditions. Similarly, within personal relationships, stigma may prevent friends, family, or colleagues from understanding or supporting someone's mental health journey, perpetuating a sense of isolation and invalidation.

The Role of Education in Reducing Stigma

Increasing Awareness through Information

Education is one of the most effective tools for combatting stigma. When people understand mental health conditions as medical issues rather than personal failings, they're more likely to approach mental health with empathy and support. Programs that provide accurate information about common conditions—such as depression, anxiety, PTSD, and bipolar disorder—help dispel myths and encourage understanding.

School and Workplace Programs

Institutions can play a pivotal role by implementing mental health education programs in schools and workplaces. These programs can teach students and employees about recognizing symptoms, seeking support, and understanding treatment options, promoting a more informed and compassionate culture.

Public Awareness Campaigns

Campaigns that destigmatize mental health reach a broad audience, using media, public figures, and storytelling to shift public attitudes. Campaigns like these often highlight stories of resilience, recovery, and hope, which counteract harmful stereotypes. By seeing people they admire openly discuss mental health, individuals may feel more empowered to seek help and share their experiences.

Advocacy: Creating Change at the Individual and Community Level

Personal Advocacy

Individuals have the power to change their minds and challenge stigma within their own circles. This could mean speaking openly about personal experiences, correcting misconceptions, or offering support to someone in need. By having honest conversations with friends, family, and colleagues, we can each play a part in creating a safer, more acceptable environment for discussing mental health.

Supporting Mental Health Organizations

Supporting mental health organizations—whether through donations, volunteering, or raising awareness—amplifies the message of acceptance and support for mental health. Many of these organizations work tirelessly to advocate for mental health policies, provide community resources, and educate the public, all of which are essential to combating stigma on a larger scale.

Legislative and Policy Advocacy

Laws and policies that protect the rights of individuals with mental health conditions are essential for reducing discrimination and improving access to care. By advocating for mental health parity, workplace protections, and increased funding for mental health services, we can support systemic changes that help normalize mental health as part of overall health.

Creating Empathy and Understanding through Personal Connections

The Power of Storytelling

Hearing personal stories of mental health challenges and recovery can humanize conditions that are often misunderstood. When people share their experiences, they help others see beyond stereotypes and recognize the resilience, hope, and courage it takes to seek help and recover. Personal stories foster empathy and can be a powerful antidote to judgment and fear.

Building Empathy through Education and Interaction

Empathy develops through understanding and experience. Encouraging interactions and relationships between people with and without mental health challenges fosters a sense of solidarity and understanding. Programs that bring communities together—through support groups, educational workshops, and public forums—allow people to engage and learn from each other's perspectives.

Practical Steps for Reducing Stigma in Daily Life

Using Respectful Language

Language shapes perceptions, and using respectful, accurate language when discussing mental health can go a long way toward reducing stigma. Phrases like "person with schizophrenia" rather than "schizophrenic" emphasize that a mental health condition is only one aspect of a person's life. Avoiding words like "crazy" or "insane" in casual conversation helps remove the negative associations that perpetuate stigma.

Encouraging Open Conversations

Normalize mental health discussions by initiating them in everyday settings, whether at home, school, or work. By addressing mental health as openly as physical health, we can reduce the taboo surrounding the topic and encourage those struggling to reach out for support.

Challenging Misconceptions

When you encounter misconceptions or stereotypes, take the opportunity to address them kindly and informatively. Educate yourself so that you can respond to misinformation with compassion and accuracy, helping to shape a more informed and accepting perspective.

The Role of Faith in Combatting Stigma

Faith-Based Communities as Allies

Faith-based communities have a unique role to play in supporting mental health and reducing stigma. When faith leaders speak openly about mental health, they help dispel myths and encourage community members to view mental health struggles as a common, human experience. By offering support, prayer, and guidance, faith communities can help individuals feel accepted and understood, rather than judged or marginalized.

Integrating Faith and Mental Health Care

For people of faith, integrating spiritual practices into mental health treatment can enhance the healing process. Many faith communities now offer counseling services, support groups, and resources that bridge mental health and spirituality. These initiatives can help reduce stigma by normalizing the experience of seeking professional support within a faith-based context.

Conclusion: Together, Breaking the Chains of Stigma

Stigma remains one of the most formidable barriers to mental health treatment, but it's a challenge that we can overcome together. Through education, empathy, advocacy, and open conversation, each of us can contribute to creating a culture that values and supports mental well-being. By breaking down stigma, we pave the way for a society where individuals feel empowered to seek help, share their struggles, and experience the full, transformative power of mental health care.

In the next chapter, we'll look at how accessible mental health care systems can serve as a foundation for lasting mental wellness, and the steps we can take to make mental health support a universal right, not a privilege.

Chapter 10: The Future of Mental Health Care

Introduction: The Growing Need for Comprehensive Mental Health Solutions

As the demand for mental health services rises, the limitations within our current mental health care system have become apparent. Many individuals lack access to services, and those who receive care often encounter hurdles such as long wait times, high costs, or inadequate support. In this chapter, we explore how we can build a sustainable mental health care system—one that not only meets current needs but adapts to future challenges and consistently prioritizes the well-being of individuals and communities.

The foundation of sustainable mental health care requires a shift in how we view mental health: as an integral aspect of overall health that deserves equal resources, support, and respect. This vision for the future of mental health care emphasizes accessibility, affordability, and quality, aiming to create a society where everyone has the resources and encouragement to seek help without fear or stigma.

Expanding Access to Mental Health Services

Increasing Access Points for Mental Health Care

One of the primary barriers to mental health care is accessibility. Many people live in areas with few mental health resources or lack the means to access services. To address this, we need to reimagine the delivery of mental

health care by increasing the variety and number of access
points:

- **Community Health Centers:** Embedding mental
  health services within community health centers can
  bring care closer to underserved populations, offering
  therapy, support groups, and screenings in familiar,
  local settings.

- **Schools and Workplaces:** Offering mental health
  support in schools and workplaces ensures that
  children, adolescents, and working adults have
  immediate access to assistance when needed. School
  counselors and workplace mental health programs
  can provide early intervention, crisis support, and
  ongoing care.

Telehealth and Digital Solutions

Digital health solutions, particularly telehealth, have become vital tools in expanding mental health care. With virtual therapy, people in rural or underserved areas, as well as those with mobility issues or busy schedules, can access care without logistical barriers. Additionally, online resources, such as mental health apps, self-help programs, and peer-support forums, empower individuals to seek guidance and learn coping skills in their own time.

Addressing Financial Barriers

For many, the cost of mental health care remains prohibitive. Insurance reforms that ensure comprehensive mental health coverage are essential to making mental health care more affordable. Sliding-scale payment models, financial assistance programs, and partnerships with non-profits can also reduce the financial burden on patients, allowing more individuals to access support.

Elevating the Quality of Mental Health Care

Training and Development for Mental Health Professionals

High-quality mental health care requires a well-trained, empathetic workforce. Ongoing education for mental health professionals ensures that they remain up to date with the latest therapeutic approaches, research, and culturally competent care practices. This is especially important for treating diverse populations, where cultural sensitivity can make a significant difference in patient outcomes.

- **Integrating Evidence-Based Practices:**

Evidence-based therapies, such as cognitive

behavioral therapy (CBT), dialectical behavior therapy

(DBT), and trauma-informed care, should be standard

across mental health practices. Ensuring that

practitioners are trained and supported in

implementing these methods promotes better

treatment outcomes and patient satisfaction.

- **Specialized Training for Complex Cases:** Some

mental health conditions, such as PTSD, severe

anxiety disorders, and personality disorders, require

specialized training. Investment in training programs

focused on complex and comorbid cases is essential to

deliver comprehensive and effective care.

Quality Measurement and Accountability

Tracking treatment outcomes, patient satisfaction, and overall care quality is essential for continual improvement. By establishing benchmarks and gathering data on patient progress, we can assess the effectiveness of different approaches and identify areas for improvement. Creating quality standards across mental health services ensures that individuals receive consistent and reliable care, regardless of where they seek treatment.

Building a Resilient and Supported Workforce

Addressing Burnout Among Mental Health Professionals

Mental health professionals are increasingly at risk for burnout due to high caseloads, emotional exhaustion, and limited resources. Supporting the well-being of these professionals is essential for a sustainable mental health system. Implementing manageable caseloads, providing regular mental health support for professionals, and fostering a culture of self-care within mental health practices are vital steps toward preventing burnout.

Increasing the Workforce

The shortage of mental health professionals in many areas contributes to long wait times and limited availability of services. Investing in mental health education programs, offering scholarships, and providing incentives for professionals to work in underserved areas can help expand the workforce. Additionally, supporting roles like peer counselors, social workers, and nurse practitioners in mental health settings can relieve some of the burden on psychiatrists and psychologists.

Integrating Mental and Physical Health Care

Collaborative Care Models

Mental and physical health are deeply interconnected, and integrating the two within a collaborative care model provides a more comprehensive approach to well-being. In this model, mental health professionals work alongside primary care providers, ensuring that individuals receive holistic care. For example, a primary care provider treating a patient with diabetes can coordinate with a mental health professional to address related depression or anxiety, leading to better overall health outcomes.

Routine Mental Health Screening

Including mental health screenings as part of regular health check-ups normalizes mental health care and can help identify issues early. Primary care providers trained to recognize mental health symptoms can refer patients to appropriate resources, catching mental health conditions before they become severe. Screening tools like the Patient Health Questionnaire (PHQ-9) for depression and the Generalized Anxiety Disorder scale (GAD-7) can be used to identify individuals who may benefit from further support.

Education for Physical Health Providers

Educating physical health providers about common mental health conditions and treatment options empowers them to advocate for their patients' mental well-being. Integrating mental health into primary care settings fosters a whole-person approach, where mental health conditions are treated with the same importance as physical ailments.

Investing in Prevention and Early Intervention

Mental Health Education Programs

Educating people about mental health from a young age promotes early awareness and reduces stigma. Schools can implement mental health curricula that teach children and adolescents about emotions, coping strategies, and when to seek help. Early education helps normalize mental health care, making it more likely for young people to recognize and address mental health challenges.

Community Support and Crisis Intervention

Community-based programs play a crucial role in preventing mental health crises. Community centers, shelters, and non-profits can offer support to those facing financial hardship, homelessness, or trauma, creating a safety net for individuals at high risk of mental health challenges. Additionally, crisis intervention services, such as suicide hotlines and mobile crisis units, provide immediate support to individuals experiencing acute distress, preventing escalation and providing a path to recovery.

Family Education and Support

Families are often the first line of support for individuals facing mental health challenges. Providing education and resources for families helps them understand mental health conditions, reduces stigma, and equips them to support their loved ones effectively. Family education programs that offer training in active listening, setting boundaries, and crisis response can be invaluable in ensuring individuals have the support they need at home.

Fostering a Culture of Empathy and Support

The Role of Public Figures and Media

Public figures who speak openly about their mental health experiences help to normalize mental health conversations. Media that accurately portrays mental health struggles and recovery can shift public perception, reducing stigma and encouraging empathy. Through documentaries, television series, and social media, the positive representation of mental health journeys empowers individuals to seek support and view mental health as an essential aspect of well-being.

Community Initiatives and Events

Community events that promote mental health awareness, such as Mental Health Awareness Month activities, support walks, and educational seminars, create spaces for people to learn, share, and connect. These events foster understanding and empathy within the community, creating an environment that embraces mental health conversations and provides support for individuals at every stage of their mental health journey.

Conclusion: Envisioning the Future of Comprehensive Mental Wellness

Building a sustainable future for mental health care requires commitment, empathy, and systemic change. By expanding access, improving care quality, supporting the workforce, and integrating mental and physical health care, we can create a future where mental health support is accessible, effective, and compassionate. A society that prioritizes mental well-being empowers individuals to live fully, fostering communities where everyone has the resources and encouragement to thrive.

In the concluding chapter, we'll reflect on the journey of mental health care and look toward a future of continual growth, compassion, and healing—a world where mental health care is recognized as an essential, universal right.

Conclusion: Charting a Path Forward in Mental Health

As we come to the close of this journey through mental health, counseling, and psychiatry, it's clear that prioritizing mental well-being is not just an individual necessity but a collective responsibility. The insights shared in this book underscore the transformative power of mental health care—not only as a means of individual healing but as a force that can shape communities, improve relationships, and drive society forward. Just as physical health enables us to work, grow, and achieve, mental health is the foundation of resilience, compassion, and purpose.

For years, misconceptions and stigmas have overshadowed the importance of mental health, deterring people from seeking help and pushing mental health challenges into the shadows. We know now that untreated mental health conditions can erode quality of life, hinder relationships, and keep individuals back from realizing their fullest potential. But through education, empathy, and accessible treatment, we can change that narrative. When individuals embrace their mental health and seek appropriate support, they can move past obstacles, find inner strength, and contribute meaningfully to the lives of others.

In this book, we examined the essential components of mental health care: the processes of counseling, the role of psychiatry, the importance of community support, and the critical value of an educated, prepared mental health workforce. We discussed the barriers that prevent so many from getting the help they need and offered potential solutions to expand access to quality care. From childhood experiences to adult challenges, each chapter has emphasized the power of seeking help and the benefits of a well-structured mental health care system. We delved into the mental health conditions that often stem from traumatic life experiences, explored the stigma surrounding mental health, and considered the systemic changes necessary for sustainable care.

As someone who has witnessed, first-hand, both the hardships and the victories in mental health care, I am deeply hopeful for the future. I have seen the lives of children, adolescents, and adults change through consistent, compassionate support, and I have seen families come together to heal. My years in advanced nursing and leadership in mental health care have affirmed my belief in the resilience of the human spirit and the impact of dedicated mental health professionals. I remain committed to advocating for all who are suffering and for those seeking paths to recovery.

As we look to the future, let this book serve as a call to action for all of us. Whether you are a person seeking support, a family member of someone struggling, or a mental health professional dedicated to helping others, know that the journey toward mental wellness is a noble one. Our collective future depends on our ability to nurture not only our own mental health but also to create an environment that fosters well-being for everyone. Mental health care is not just for those experiencing a crisis; it is a resource for all stages of life and a foundation upon which every individual can build.

Let us work together to dismantle stigma, to uplift those in need, and to build a world where mental health care is universally respected, accessible, and cherished. With God's guidance, our shared commitment to compassion, and our dedication to growth, we can shape a society that fully understands, values, and protects mental health. The journey is far from over, but by embracing the tools and insights outlined in these pages, we are one step closer to a world where everyone has the opportunity to live with purpose, connection, and peace of mind.

Thank you for embarking on this journey with me. Let us move forward with hope, courage, and a commitment to a healthier, more understanding world. Together, we can make a difference that will echo across generations.

Appendix: Additional Resources and Recommended Reading

1. Foundational Resources for Mental Health

To support readers in gaining a broader understanding of mental health, counseling, and psychiatry, the following foundational resources offer accessible information and guidance. These sources include online platforms, helplines, and organizations dedicated to mental health education and advocacy.

- **National Alliance on Mental Illness (NAMI)**

  Website: www.nami.org

  NAMI provides a wide range of resources, including educational materials, support groups, and advocacy programs for individuals living with mental health conditions and their families. Their "Basics" education program, designed specifically for caregivers of children and adolescents, is especially useful for those seeking practical knowledge on managing mental health in loved ones.

- **Mental Health America (MHA)**

Website: www.mhanational.org

MHA offers resources on early intervention, mental health screenings, and public health advocacy. Their tools, including online mental health tests, can be valuable for those seeking an initial understanding of mental health challenges and resources to support ongoing well-being.

- **Substance Abuse and Mental Health Services Administration (SAMHSA)**

  Website: www.samhsa.gov

  SAMHSA's mission is to improve access to mental health and substance use disorder services. The organization provides a comprehensive treatment locator, information on funding for community mental health initiatives, and an extensive list of guides on specific conditions and treatments.

- **National Institute of Mental Health (NIMH)**

  Website: www.nimh.nih.gov

  The NIMH offers in-depth research and educational resources on a variety of mental health conditions. It is an excellent resource for those interested in the scientific and medical aspects of mental health and ongoing research in psychiatry.

2. Faith and Mental Health Resources

For readers who, like me, draw strength from their faith, the following resources bridge spirituality and mental well-being. Faith-based mental health resources can provide guidance that aligns with both mental health care principles and spiritual beliefs.

- **American Association of Christian Counselors (AACC)**

  Website: www.aacc.net

  The AACC is dedicated to supporting Christian mental health professionals and the faith-based counseling community. Their resources, conferences, and training materials are rooted in Christian principles and provide a supportive community for mental health professionals and individuals seeking faith-aligned guidance.

- **Focus on the Family – Christian Counseling Resources**

Website: www.focusonthefamily.com

This organization offers articles, podcasts, and counseling resources aimed at integrating Christian faith with mental health support. Focus on the Family provides valuable materials for those looking to navigate mental health issues through a faith-based lens, including advice on family mental health dynamics and personal well-being.

3. Recommended Reading: Books on Mental Health, Counseling, and Psychiatry

For those who seek a deeper understanding of mental health principles, counseling techniques, or psychiatric approaches, the following books serve as valuable resources:

- **The Healing Path: Understanding the Power of Counseling and Psychiatry** by Aaron Esfahani, MSN, APRN, BSBA

  This prior work delves into the healing potential of counseling and psychiatry, offering readers insight into various therapeutic methods and the vital role of professional support in mental health. It's an ideal complement to *The Essential Guide to Mental Health* and provides an in-depth look at how counseling and psychiatry foster growth, resilience, and personal transformation.

- **Feeling Good: The New Mood Therapy** by Dr. David D. Burns

  Known as a seminal work on cognitive behavioral therapy (CBT), this book offers practical techniques for identifying and changing negative thought patterns. For those looking to engage in self-guided mental health support, Dr. Burns' approach is straightforward and empowering.

- **The Body Keeps the Score: Brain, Mind, and Body in the Healing of Trauma** by Dr. Bessel van der Kolk

  This groundbreaking work provides a comprehensive look at trauma and its impact on the body and mind.

Dr. van der Kolk explores trauma recovery and discusses both traditional and innovative therapeutic approaches, making it a valuable resource for anyone dealing with trauma personally or professionally.

- **Grace for the Afflicted: A Clinical and Biblical Perspective on Mental Illness** by Dr. Matthew S. Stanford

Integrating mental health science with Christian faith, Dr. Stanford's book explores mental health conditions from both a clinical and biblical perspective. This work is an insightful resource for individuals or families who want to understand mental health conditions in a way that resonates with their faith.

- **Lost Connections: Uncovering the Real Causes of Depression – and the Unexpected Solutions**

by Johann Hari

This thought-provoking book challenges common perceptions of depression, exploring social, environmental, and lifestyle factors that influence mental health. Hari's perspective on depression and holistic healing provides readers with a broader understanding of mental well-being.

---

4. Self-Care and Wellness Resources

For those looking to incorporate self-care practices that support mental health, the following tools and resources are particularly beneficial:

- **Headspace and Calm**

  These mindfulness and meditation apps offer guided exercises to help users reduce stress, improve focus, and enhance emotional well-being. With options for both beginners and experienced practitioners, these apps are accessible tools for integrating mindfulness into daily routines.

- **Mindfulness-Based Stress Reduction (MBSR) Programs**

  Originating from the work of Dr. Jon Kabat-Zinn, MBSR is a structured program that combines mindfulness and yoga to help people manage stress, anxiety, and chronic pain. Online MBSR courses are widely available, making it easy to engage in this practice from home.

- **Mental Health First Aid**

  Website: www.mentalhealthfirstaid.org

  Mental Health First Aid provides courses that teach participants how to identify, understand, and respond to mental health crises. This program is valuable for individuals interested in being proactive about mental health awareness within their communities, families, or workplaces.

---

5. Crisis Resources and Immediate Support

If you or someone you know is experiencing a mental health crisis, the following resources provide immediate, confidential support:

- **National Suicide Prevention Lifeline**

  Phone: 988 (U.S. only)

This lifeline provides free and confidential support 24/7, offering help for individuals in crisis or distress. It's an essential resource for those who may not know where else to turn during difficult times.

- **Crisis Text Line**

  Text: HELLO to 741741 (U.S. and Canada)

  The Crisis Text Line offers support via text message, which can be an accessible and non-intrusive way for people in distress to reach out for help.

- **National Domestic Violence Hotline**

  Phone: 1-800-799-SAFE (7233) (U.S. only)

  For those experiencing abuse, this hotline provides resources, support, and safe solutions. Mental health is closely linked to domestic safety, and access to

resources for protection and empowerment is
essential.

Conclusion of Appendix

Incorporating mental health support into our lives goes
beyond self-help—it's a journey that requires reliable
resources, expert guidance, and a supportive community.
The resources listed here are intended to empower you,
whether you are navigating your own mental health
journey or supporting someone else. Remember, mental
health is a fundamental aspect of well-being, and accessing
these tools can make a profound difference in anyone's
life.

May these resources, along with the insights from *The
Essential Guide to Mental Health*, inspire you to pursue

growth, seek help when needed, and contribute to a more

compassionate and understanding world.